Riddles of the Universe

John Bonallack

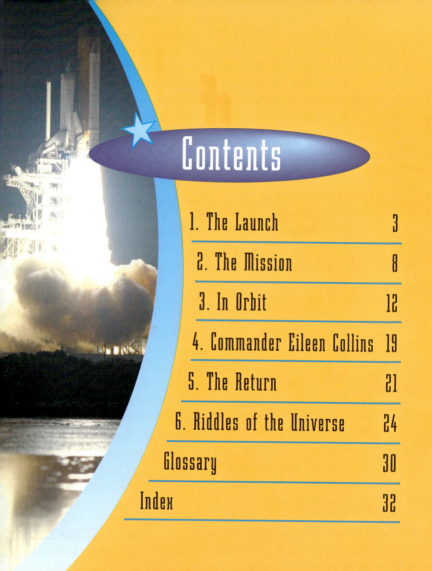

Contents

1. The Launch	3
2. The Mission	8
3. In Orbit	12
4. Commander Eileen Collins	19
5. The Return	21
6. Riddles of the Universe	24
Glossary	30
Index	32

1. The Launch

20 July 1999. Kennedy Space Center, Florida. Commander Eileen Collins and her crew board the **space shuttle** *Columbia*. Their mission: to launch the $1.6 billion ***Chandra*** X-ray Observatory.

Five minutes to go. *(Close helmet visors.)*

The countdown begins. Ten … nine … *(Deep breaths, try to relax.)* eight … seven … STOP!

The computers show that there is too much **hydrogen** fuel around the main engine. The launch is terminated, a split second before the main engines are set to fire.

22 July. The launch is called off again – this time because of thunderstorms over Kennedy Space Center.

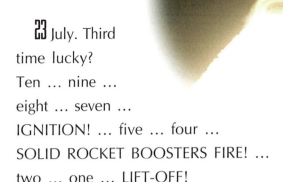

23 July. Third time lucky? Ten … nine … eight … seven … IGNITION! … five … four … SOLID ROCKET BOOSTERS FIRE! … two … one … LIFT-OFF!

Columbia rises slowly off the pad, a huge fireball at its tail. The noise is incredible. The shuttle shudders with the enormous thrust of the **solid rocket boosters** (SRBs). The astronauts are forced back into their seats by three **G**s of acceleration – that's three times the force of **gravity**. Two minutes later, the solid rocket boosters fall away like spent skyrockets, their work done.

The stages of take-off

1. The space shuttle is launched by three main engines and two solid rocket boosters.
2. The SRBs are discarded at a height of about 45 kilometres.
3. The SRBs parachute down to the sea and are picked up by ship.
4. The external fuel tank is discarded when it is almost empty.
5. The tank breaks up in the atmosphere and falls into the sea.
6. The shuttle is propelled into orbit by its orbital manoeuvring engines.

The main engines continue the work. But there's a problem – hydrogen fuel is leaking. Will there be enough to get the shuttle out into **orbit**?

And now another problem – two of the six computers that control the main engines crash.

Somewhere in all those kilometres of wiring, there is a short circuit. If one more computer fails, the engines will shut down. Commander Collins and Pilot Jeff Ashby get ready to make a risky landing in Africa if they need to.

But the remaining systems keep going. Five minutes … seven minutes … eight and a half minutes … the engines stop. A tonne of fuel has leaked away, and the fuel tank is exhausted, but there is just enough for the shuttle to reach orbit. The mission can go on.

Crew of the Chandra mission (STS-93)

Steve Hawley: *Mission Specialist*

Jeffrey Ashby: *Pilot*

Michel Tognini: *Mission Specialist*

Eileen Collins: *Commander*

Catherine (Cady) Coleman: *Mission Specialist*

2. The Mission

There are many questions about space that cannot be answered using visible-light telescopes based on Earth. Dust and the air itself distort their view. Even orbiting telescopes like **Hubble** are unable to see some things. To see what is happening near **black holes** or to see stars that are billions of light years away, we need an orbiting telescope that can detect x-rays. The telescope's orbit needs to be beyond the **radiation belt** that surrounds Earth so that it can get a clear view of the universe.

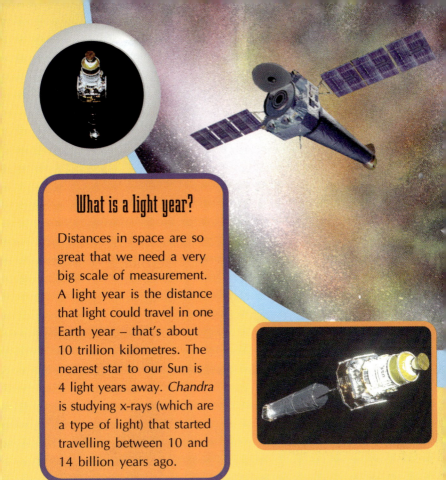

What is a light year?

Distances in space are so great that we need a very big scale of measurement. A light year is the distance that light could travel in one Earth year – that's about 10 trillion kilometres. The nearest star to our Sun is 4 light years away. *Chandra* is studying x-rays (which are a type of light) that started travelling between 10 and 14 billion years ago.

Chandra is the world's most powerful telescope, built into a spacecraft, with its own rocket engines and fuel tanks. It is about 14 metres long and weighs over 5000 kilograms.

Once it has been released into space, *Chandra*'s rocket engines will blast it into an orbit that will take it a third of the way to the Moon. It will have 55 hours of clear viewing in each 64-hour orbit of Earth. It can detect faint x-rays from stars that are 10 to 14 billion light years away – which is like looking back in time, almost to the beginning of the universe. *Chandra* will be able to study particles right up until the last second before they are sucked into a black hole.

An image made by Chandra *of the remains of an exploded star*

How fast do sound and light travel?

Have a friend stand about 100 metres away from you and clap two boards together. You will see the boards hit and then hear the sound a split second later. This is because light travels much faster than sound – nearly a million times faster. In one second, sound travels about a third of a kilometre. In the same period of time, light can travel a distance equal to seven times around the world.

Chandra's orbit

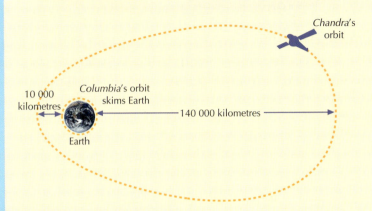

Columbia orbits 290 kilometres above Earth, at a speed of 29 000 kilometres per hour. It takes 90 minutes to complete an orbit.

Chandra has an **elliptical** orbit that brings it within 10 000 kilometres of Earth and out again to 143 000 kilometres, every 64 hours. It speeds up and slows down at different parts of the orbit but averages about 6500 kilometres per hour.

3. In Orbit

Chandra is the largest and heaviest **payload** ever carried by a space shuttle. How do you lift a 23 000-kilogram, 14-metre spacecraft out of a shuttle's payload bay? – Very carefully! Mission Specialists Michel Tognini and Cady Coleman operate the robotic arm to gently, slowly lift *Chandra* out.

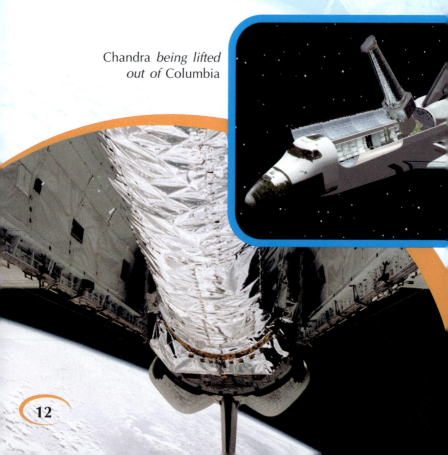

Chandra *being lifted out of* Columbia

Next, Commander Collins moves *Columbia* away to a safe distance so that *Chandra* can blast into a higher orbit without damaging the shuttle. Ground crew back on Earth take over control to fire *Chandra*'s rockets, and it moves out into space.

Once *Chandra* is safely away, Eileen and her crew get on with their other tasks and with day-to-day life in space. All five crew members are experienced astronauts. Their training in preparation for this mission has been intensive. They have practised the tasks they are to carry out in space in dive tanks, wearing **scuba** gear. This is as close as you can get to **zero gravity** conditions on Earth.

The crew are busy most of the time – doing general housekeeping, preparing meals, stowing rubbish, cleaning and changing air filters, taking photographs, and writing and sending reports back to Earth. There are also the official experiments to complete.

Every task in zero gravity is more tricky than on Earth. Foot restraints in the floor keep the crew in place as they work, and **Velcro** tabs anchor things. Even so, the astronauts have to consider every move carefully so that they don't bounce off the cabin walls and ceiling or let food crumbs or blobs of drink float into the delicate instruments.

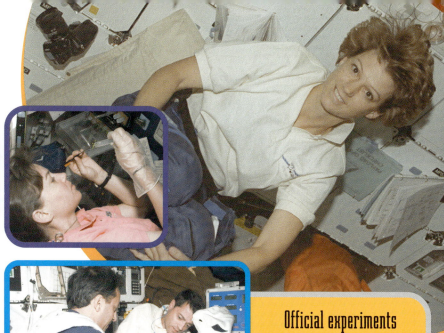

Official experiments

The deployment of *Chandra* was the main mission for Commander Collins and her crew, but they also carried out a number of other experiments and tasks while in orbit, including:

- testing new types of lightweight hinges for solar panels on spacecraft
- conducting an experiment designed to help amateur radio enthusiasts communicate directly with shuttle crews
- test-firing the shuttle's engines
- growing plants and cells in zero gravity
- testing a vibration-free exercise treadmill for astronauts to use aboard the International Space Station (see page 18).

Day and night don't mean much when you're orbiting Earth every 90 minutes. But the crew keep a normal Earth routine, with regular meals, and eight hours' sleep in every twenty-four. In zero gravity, the bunks can be anywhere – even on the walls or the ceiling! But the astronauts have to be Velcroed to their bunks so they don't float away. The spent air they breathe out in their sleep is blown away with air jets so that they don't suffocate. Astronauts wash themselves with a sponge (you can't have a shower in zero gravity) and use a special toilet with a suction tube that carries away the waste.

Astronauts choose their own menus from a wide variety of **freeze-dried** food. Meals are **reconstituted** by injecting hot or cold water into a packet, then making a slit in it to insert a spoon. They also carry some fresh foods. Astronauts' favourite foods include prawn cocktail with sauce, tortillas with peanut butter and cheese spreads, chicken dishes, sweets, biscuits, chewing gum, and apples.

Space shuttle crew members can take up to 20 small personal items on board with them in their "personal preference kit". They are limited to 1 kilogram in a container about the size of a chocolate box. Most astronauts take cameras, sweets, family photos, and letters. Commander Collins also took along a scarf and pilot's licence that belonged to pioneer aviator **Amelia Earhart**.

The International Space Station

This project, led by the United States, involves 16 countries. When complete, the space station will serve as a laboratory in space and a gateway to space exploration. Crews of up to seven people will live and work there for up to 6 months. The space station will consist of a number of modules (separate parts), which are launched separately and assembled in space. It will take 5 years and more than 50 space flights to launch the modules.

4. Commander Eileen Collins

Eileen Collins was born in New York in 1956. She is "a very ordinary, down-to-earth person" her parents say. "Nobody handed her anything. Everything she is today, she's earned."

As a child, her favourite TV programmes were *Star Trek* and *Lost in Space*. At high school, she started reading about famous pilots such as Amelia Earhart. "Their stories inspired me," she says. "I admired the courage of those women to go and fly into dangerous situations."

While at university, Eileen worked part-time to pay for flying lessons. After graduating, she went straight into the Air Force. That was when she decided to become an astronaut.

Just 5 years later, she became the first woman to pilot a space shuttle, as part of the Russian-American space programme, and visited the **Mir space station**. In 1997, Eileen spent 9 days in space, travelling 145 times around the earth – that's 6 500 000 kilometres.

In 1999, Eileen became the first woman to command a space shuttle. On her appointment, she said, "When I was a child, I dreamed about space. I admired pilots and astronauts, and I've admired explorers of all kinds. It was only a dream that I would someday be one of them. It is my hope that all children … will be inspired to reach for their dreams – because dreams do come true!"

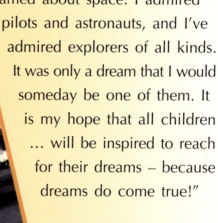

5. The Return

On the fourth day in space, Commander Collins and her crew begin packing up their experiments and fastening everything back in its proper place. Eileen and Pilot Jeff Ashby check the instruments and test-fire the steering jets.

It's time. Eileen and Jeff turn the space shuttle so that it is travelling tail-first. Now, they fire the jets to slow the shuttle a little. Gravity starts pulling it back to Earth.

Michel Tognini prepares for Columbia's descent

Eileen's husband and daughter wait for her to land safely

The streak left behind Columbia as it re-ent the atmosphere over Mexico

Nine thousand metres from the ground, Eileen takes control. As the shuttle passes over Mexico and Florida, observers on the ground see a fiery streak and then hear the **sonic boom**. Eileen glides the shuttle in to land at Kennedy Space Center, Cape Canaveral. It has been just under 5 days since take-off, but it seems like a year. So much has happened – so much has been accomplished.

Word comes from Mission Control:

"Welcome home, Eileen. To you and your crew, just an outstanding job!"

As soon as the crew leaves the shuttle, technicians start going over it. They find that a metal plug is missing from one of the tubes in the engine, and there are holes in three of the liquid hydrogen tubes where the plug blasted across them. The next task is to examine the wiring to see what crashed the shuttle's engine computers. They find a short circuit between a worn wire and a screw head – a small thing, but it was almost enough to make the engines fail during the launch.

But right now, this is not Commander Collins's problem. As soon as the welcome speeches and autograph signing are over, she will be on her way home, another mission completed.

6. Riddles of the Universe

Astronomers are excited about the images coming back from *Chandra*. The x-ray telescope is getting down to serious work – probing black holes, studying **supernovas**, and looking for **dark matter**.

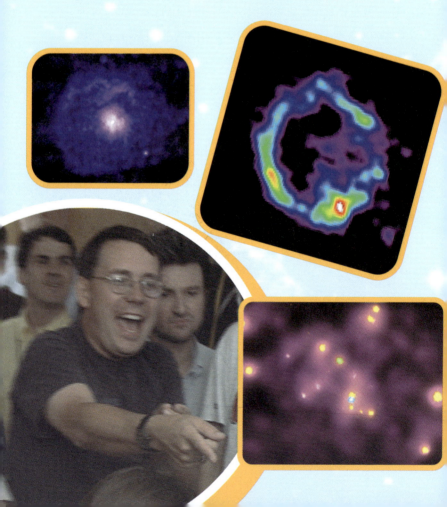

What are black holes?

A star is a huge and continuous nuclear explosion that is held together by its colossal gravity. But when a star runs out of nuclear fuel, it collapses in on itself, crushing even its own atoms. A small-to-medium star, like our Sun, eventually becomes a white dwarf – a dead, incredibly dense lump of matter.

The collapse of a bigger star creates a black hole, which has gravity so powerful that not even light can escape. This means that we have no way of seeing what black holes look like.

An artist's impression of a black hole

Astronomers believe that there are super-massive black holes, formed from billions of collapsed stars, at the centre of galaxies. Stars in our own **galaxy**, the Milky Way, may be swirling round one of these black holes, like boats in a giant whirlpool, gradually being sucked in and gobbled up. (We are talking billions of years here, not next week!)

By locating black holes and observing activity at the very edge of them, *Chandra* may provide some new clues to the nature of these fascinating space mysteries.

What are supernovas?

As a star collapses, it creates one last brilliant explosion. This blasts heavy atoms such as carbon and oxygen out into the universe. Without supernovas releasing these elements, planets that are able to support life, like Earth, could not have formed. Images from *Chandra*, which provide up to 50 times more detail than those from any earlier x-ray telescope, will help astronomers to study supernovas.

What is dark matter?

X-ray pictures from outer space reveal masses of very hot gas throughout the galaxies. Astronomers have worked out that the total gravity of all the galaxies isn't enough to stop this gas spreading out – yet it doesn't spread. Something must be providing the gravity that keeps it together – something that weighs more than all the stars and all the gases in the whole universe! Astronomers have never seen this something, but they have given it a name: dark matter.

Chandra will map the locations of dark matter and help scientists to find out what it is. If *Chandra* can help to solve this mystery, it may provide clues about how the universe began, how it has evolved, and what might become of it.

Fun facts about Chandra

- *Chandra* is the world's most powerful x-ray telescope – so powerful, it is like reading a newspaper a kilometre away.

- *Chandra* can observe sources 200 times fainter than any previous x-ray telescope was able to detect.

- Some of the x-rays observed by *Chandra* have been travelling through space at the speed of light for 14 billion years.

- The mirrors of the *Chandra* telescope are aligned with the same accuracy as a golfer would need to hit a hole-in-one from 200 kilometres away.

- *Chandra* flies 200 times higher than the *Hubble* telescope – more than a third of the way to the moon on each orbit.

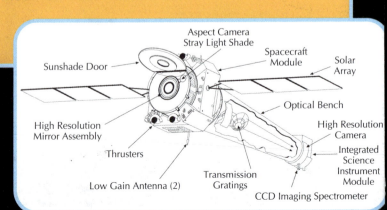

Chandra on the net

You can find out more about *Chandra* on the Internet. Try searching under "Chandra X-ray Observatory". Scroll through the matches and choose one that seems to cover what you want – for example, "Chandra X-ray Observatory Center – Public Information and Education" (http://xrtpub.harvard.edu/pub.html). Other useful keywords are "STS-93", "NASA", and "space shuttle".

Glossary

(These words are printed in bold type
the first time they appear in the book.)

Amelia Earhart: a pioneer aviator who disappeared in 1937 while trying to fly solo around the world

astronomer: a scientist who studies stars and space

black hole: the collapsed form of a large star at the end of its life

Chandra: the x-ray telescope named after Subrahmanyan Chandrasekhar, an Indian astronomer and winner of the Nobel Prize in 1983

dark matter: matter that is believed to exist in space in massive amounts but has never been seen

elliptical: in the shape of an ellipse – rather like the outline of an egg

freeze-dried: food dried by freezing rather than heating

G: acceleration equal to the force of gravity, which is the pressure you feel when a car you are in accelerates or turns sharply

galaxy: a large system of stars held together by gravity

gravity: the pull of any mass towards any other mass

Hubble: an orbiting space telescope that was launched in 1990 to study distant stars

hydrogen: one of the ingredients of rocket fuel

Glossary

Mir space station: the space laboratory put into orbit by Russia in 1986

orbit: the fixed path of a planet or satellite circling a larger body

payload: the load that a vehicle can carry, including people and cargo but not including fuel and essential equipment

radiation belt: a belt of electrically charged atoms that circles Earth

reconstituted: returned to its original state

scuba: underwater breathing equipment worn by divers

solid rocket boosters: two solid-fuel rockets attached to a shuttle to boost it out into orbit

sonic boom: the explosion of sound created when an aircraft travels faster than the speed of sound (about 1200 kilometres per hour)

space shuttle: a shuttle is something that goes back and forth; space shuttles (like *Columbia*) go back and forth between Earth and space

supernova: the explosion of a star at the end of its life

Velcro: a reusable fastener that joins by using tiny hooks and loops

zero gravity: the state of weightlessness that exists in space

Index

Ashby, Jeffrey	6, 7, 21	dark matter	24, 27
astronauts	7, 12–18	gravity	5, 21
bunks	16	zero gravity	13, 14, 16
food	17	Hawley, Steve	7
personal preference kits	18	*Hubble* space telescope	8, 28
tasks in space	14–15	hydrogen	4
training	13	International Space Station	15, 18
black holes	8, 10, 24–26	Kennedy Space Center	4, 22
Chandra X-ray Observatory	9	light, speed of	10
fun facts about	28	light years	8, 9
information sought by	10, 24–27	Mir Space Station	20
orbit	10, 11, 28	Mission Control	13, 22
Coleman, Catherine (Cady)	7, 12	radiation belt	8
Collins, Eileen	3, 6, 13, 21–23	sound, speed of	10
early life	19–20	sonic boom	22
Columbia		supernova	24, 26
launch	3–7	Tognini, Michel	7, 12, 21
orbit	6, 11, 16	x-rays	8, 9, 28
payload	12		
return to Earth	21–23		